APPLE CID

150+ Amazing and Surprising Uses for Apple Cider Vinegar to Heal your Body Inside and Out. Essential Recipes for ACV Miracle Health System

_____

JANET HATCH

Thank you for choosing this book

I wish you a good read and

If you like, leave a short review on Amazon.

Thank You!

Table of Contents

Introduction

Until now, you may have thought that apple cider vinegar is only good for dressing salads. But people across the globe use apple cider vinegar in a number of other, more medicinal ways.

In fact, many even use it as the central ingredient in what's called an apple cider vinegar detox.

The idea behind the detox is that raw, unfiltered apple cider vinegar still has "the mother" in it. The mother contains good bacteria for the gut, vitamins, minerals, and enzymes. It's normal for apple cider vinegar with the mother to be murky or cloudy.

The use of apple cider vinegar for detoxification, diet, or other benefits goes back thousands of years. Some even claim the father of medicine, Hippocrates, promoted its health qualities as far back as 400 B.C.

More recently, makers of Bragg apple cider vinegar have been touting its health advantages since 1912.

The body is able to detoxify itself. There isn't much scientific research to support the argument that detox diets remove toxins from the body.

Many people use a detox diet to begin changing their diet, removing processed foods and introducing healthier whole foods.

The supposed benefits you may gain from an apple cider vinegar detox are both internal and external. They include:

- giving the body a good dose of enzymes
- increasing potassium intake
- supporting a healthy immune system
- helping with weight control
- promoting pH balance in the body
- aiding with healthy digestion
- adding good bacteria for the gut and immune function
- helping remove "sludge toxins" from the body
- soothing skin and helping keep it healthy
- healing acne when used externally

You may hear that apple cider vinegar helps reduce appetite and even burn fat. There's also evidence to suggest that adding apple cider vinegar to your daily routine may help with type 2 diabetes and high cholesterol.

How to do an apple cider vinegar detox

The basic recipe is as follows:

- 1 to 2 tablespoons of raw, unfiltered apple cider vinegar
- 8 ounces of purified or distilled water
- 1 to 2 tablespoons sweetener (organic honey, maple syrup, or 4 drops of Stevia)

There are many variations of this basic drink. Some include adding lemon juice. Others add a dash of cayenne pepper.

With an apple cider vinegar detox, you consume this type of drink regularly for a set period of time — several days to a month or more.

Many people choose to consume it three times each day: upon waking, midmorning, and again midafternoon.

It should be noted that there isn't any formal research specifically about apple cider vinegar as part of a detox diet.

Much of the information you'll find around is purely anecdotal. Read it with caution. But this isn't to say that the health properties of apple cider vinegar haven't been examined.

For example, there's a growing body of research related to apple cider vinegar and its impact on type 2 diabetes.

In one small study, consuming this ingredient lowered both blood glucose and insulin in 12 participants with diabetes. Not only that, but the participants' fullness after eating bread increased.

When it comes to weight loss, there are a few studies that support apple cider vinegar's powers.

One study revealed that obese rats who drank apple cider vinegar daily lost more body weight and fat mass than the rats in the control group. The waist circumference and triglyceride levels for rats in the groups that consumed apple cider vinegar lowered significantly as well.

In yet another study, apple cider vinegar lowered the LDL, triglyceride, and cholesterol levels in 19 people with hyperlipidemia, or high blood fats.

The results suggest that regularly consuming apple cider vinegar may be a good way to prevent atherosclerosis for people at high risk of developing this complication and other heart issues.

However, these studies were either conducted on animals or very small sample groups of people. Larger-scale studies on humans are still needed.

So, this you need to know before you start guzzling lots of apple cider vinegar, make sure it's diluted with water. Apple cider vinegar in its pure form is acidic. It may erode tooth enamel or even burn your mouth and throat.

If you do choose to do the detox, be sure to rinse your mouth with water after drinking the vinegar. You may even want to drink it through a straw. Even just one glass a day may be enough to negatively affect your teeth.

Apple cider vinegar may also interact with different medications or supplements. In particular, it may contribute to low potassium levels if you take diuretics or insulin.

If you take diuretics or insulin, talk to your doctor before you start consuming apple cider vinegar regularly or try the detox.

People who have tried an apple cider detox do share that you may have some nausea or stomach discomfort after drinking it. This discomfort is usually worse in the morning hours when your stomach is empty.

So, while there isn't a huge body of research to suggest apple cider vinegar is a miracle health cure, the testimonials and reviews you'll find online can be compelling.

Trying an apple cider vinegar detox is likely safe for most people.

In the end, the best way to "detox" your body may be to stop taking in sugars and processed foods and eat a healthy diet rich in whole foods, like fresh fruits and vegetables, whole grains, and lean proteins.

If you're still interested in apple cider vinegar, it's a good idea to check with your doctor before adding this ingredient to your diet. This is especially so if you're taking medications or supplements.

CHAPTER 1

19 Benefits of Drinking Apple Cider Vinegar & How To Drink It

Lately, everybody seems to be saying apple cider vinegar is amazing and it has so many health benefits. Wanna know why and what those benefits are, specifically? Here are all the reasons why everyone is drinking apple cider vinegar plus helpful tips for how to incorporate apple cider vinegar to your diet.

Apple cider vinegar is everywhere. Everybody talks about it and everybody seems to love it. Is this just a new hype or is apple cider vinegar actually amazing? Are there actual health benefits of apple cider vinegar?

First of all, there's nothing new here. Apple cider vinegar was used as a natural remedy for health problems for a very long period of time. In fact, it's an ancient remedy. It seems that we're becoming more aware of those benefits these days, but they were always there. It's a re-discovery, if you will.

More people are trying to improve their life by making healthier and more natural choices these days and that's why you'll see apple cider vinegar pretty much anywhere there's a conversation about health, food, and natural remedies.

So I'll get my POV right out here: I think Apple Cider Vinegar (aka ACV) is amazing. Seriously, Amazing.

And most of the health benefits of apple cider vinegar are endorsed by science — so nope, not just a hype.

However, despite being so amazing, apple cider vinegar won't work miracles. And it won't replace a balanced diet and exercise. It promotes health and it helps you maintain it but drinking apple cider vinegar won't have a major impact unless you're making other steps towards your health. No remedy can do that. Moderation is always key.

What Is Apple Cider Vinegar?

Apple cider vinegar is a type of vinegar made from apples. Duh, right? More specifically, it's fermented apple juice.

To make apple cider vinegar, apples are crushed and exposed to yeast. By doing this, the natural sugar from the apple is fermented over time and turned into alcohol (like you would do with wine). Sounds like making apple cider, right? Yeah, because the process is similar. The difference is the apple cider vinegar is fermented twice –once to make alcoholic cider and a second time to make it vinegar.

Why Drink Apple Cider Vinegar?

As crazy as it may sound at first, drinking apple cider vinegar will bring you many health benefits which will be discussed in detail in just a sec. Aside from health benefits, apple cider vinegar also reduces cravings by inducing satiety which means apple cider vinegar is great for weight loss or for maintaining a healthy lifestyle. Not only that, but apple cider vinegar is filled with beneficial nutrients.

basically, apple cider vinegar rocks!

Health Benefits of Apple Cider Vinegar

So what about those health benefits of apple cider vinegar? This almost-magical vinegar can do many things for your health. Let's start with a list and then get into more details with the ones that will help you to live a healthier life, ok?

Apple cider vinegar...

- is a natural laxative and it can improve digestion;
- lowers blood sugar levels;
- improves insulin sensitivity;
- increases satiety and helps people to lose weight;
- reduces belly fat;
- lowers cholesterol;
- lowers blood pressure and improves heart health;
- prevents and decreases the risk of getting cancer and slows down the growth of cancer cells.

Helpful Nutrients in Apple Cider Vinegar

Impressive, right? But wait... there's more. Apple cider vinegar is also a nutritional powerhouse. That would explain some of the health benefits! Let's take a closer look at apple cider vinegar's nutritional composition to see what makes it so special.

Apple cider vinegar contains:

- magnesium;
- iron;
- phosphorus;
- manganese;
- amino acids;
- antioxidants;
- only 3 calories per tablespoon.

Drinking Apple Cider Vinegar for Weight Loss

Most people use apple cider vinegar for weight loss, but they don't know the rest of the health benefits of apple cider vinegar. That's because apple cider vinegar was used as an aid in weight loss for ages.

There are several studies that have concluded using apple cider vinegar for weight loss actually works. They also found it works even without dietary changes. However, when drinking apple cider combined with a healthy lifestyle, the results are truly impressive.

So, how does this happen? Most people overeat because they don't feel full. Apple cider vinegar increases satiety (your feeling of fullness) and that's very helpful for staying on track with your healthy diet. Especially at the beginning of your weight loss journey when you need a little bit of help to start and to stay on track.

Apple Cider Vinegar and Diabetes

When it comes to apple cider vinegar and diabetes, there are a few things you should know. Apple cider vinegar is great in diabetes prevention. So, if you have a family history of diabetes, you should consider drinking apple cider vinegar to decrease the risk.

Apple cider vinegar has been shown to reduce blood sugar levels when one is fasting (not eating), which is incredibly beneficial for people who have difficulty regulating their own blood sugar levels, like those who have diabetes. However, this won't replace medication.

A healthy diet and exercise are always recommended for people with diabetes. If you have diabetes and take insulin or prescription drugs, you should talk to your doctor before drinking apple cider vinegar because your potassium levels can drop too much.

Cholesterol, Blood Pressure, and Apple Cider Vinegar

Other common uses for apple cider vinegar are to lower blood pressure and reduce cholesterol levels. What's the deal with apple cider vinegar cholesterol and apple cider vinegar blood pressure? Apple cider vinegar helps in controlling renin, a hormone produces by your kidneys that is responsible for constricting and dilating the blood vessels. When the blood vessels are constricting, the blood pressure rises. Apple cider vinegar keeps the vessels relax, and that means blood pressure won't rise.

As for apple cider vinegar helping with cholesterol – drinking apple cider vinegar before a meal lowers cholesterol. Basically, studies have shown that apple cider vinegar reduces LDL (bad cholesterol) and increases HDL (good cholesterol) due to its natural antioxidants.

How Apple Cider Vinegar Helps with Digestion

As I already mentioned, apple cider vinegar improves digestion. Drinking apple cider vinegar for digestion can do the following:

- get rid of heartburn;
- reduce bloating;
- improve digestion overall.

Let me just say that discomfort and pain are not normal. When we experience pain and discomfort after a meal, we should listen to our bodies and realize that something is not exactly right. Maybe we ate too much or maybe our digestive system doesn't work properly.

Proper digestion means proper acid levels in the stomach so the nutrients in our food can be absorbed. When there's not enough acid, food is not properly broken down and the nutrients are not assimilated which can lead to digestive issues like the ones I mentioned. Or more serious ones.

Drinking apple cider vinegar for digestion means increasing acid production. And that leads to proper digestion. Simple, right?

Apple Cider Vinegar Kills Bacteria

Did you know apple cider vinegar kills bacteria? In fact, apple cider vinegar was used for disinfecting wounds and treating fungus back in the day.

It was – and still is – a great way to treat and prevent infection because apple cider vinegar can kill bacteria easily. It also inhibits bacteria, like E-coli, from spoiling food so that's why it's so often used as a food preservative. It's also natural and better than artificial preservatives. So awesome!

Apple Cider Vinegar and Cancer

When it comes to apple cider vinegar and cancer, it has been shown that apple cider vinegar can help in cancer prevention because it promotes health. There are many factors and causes for cancer and we still have a long way to go in terms of prevention and treatment but, what we do know is apple cider vinegar can reduce the risk of cancer and can slow down the cancer cell (tumor) growth.

That being said, apple cider vinegar shouldn't replace treatment for someone diagnosed with cancer or a healthy lifestyle for those who want to reduce the risk of developing different types of cancer.

Using Apple Cider Vinegar for Skin and Hair

Aside from the health benefits of apple cider vinegar, using apple cider vinegar can also improve skin appearance and hair health. Woot! See? Apple cider vinegar is indeed amazing. Told ya!

Why apple cider vinegar is great for skin and hair:

- treats and reduces the prevalence of acne;
- treats and soothes sunburn;
- has anti-aging properties;
- improves hair health;
- combats hair tangles;
- reduces hair frizz;

- seals the hair cuticles and help the hair to retain moisture;
- treats dandruff.

Seriously, is there anything apple cider vinegar cannot do? I don't think so! However, it's important to note it is not recommended to apply apple cider vinegar to the skin without diluting it in water first.

Popular Ways to Drink Apple Cider Vinegar

Since there are so many health benefits apple of cider vinegar, you're probably considering drinking apple cider vinegar right out of the bottle to benefit from its amazing properties. But let's first discuss how to drink apple cider vinegar.

First off, look for the unfiltered and organic type because that's the best type.

How to drink apple cider vinegar

Well, you don't really have to drink it. Especially if you don't like the taste. There are other ways to consume apple cider vinegar. You can incorporate apple cider vinegar into your diet by;

- using it in various recipes including salad dressing recipes and marinade recipes.
- making an apple cider vinegar tonic by mixing apple cider vinegar with lemon juice – 2 tablespoons of apple cider vinegar added to a glass of fruit juice. Drinking apple cider vinegar is easier this way. You won't notice the taste as much but you'll get all the health benefits of apple cider. Plus the benefits of fruit juice. Make your own fruit juice at home for a fresh and yummy tonic. You can spice it up with a little ground cinnamon or cayenne pepper or sweeten it with a little raw honey. Good stuff.

If you don't mind the taste of apple cider vinegar, you can add it to a glass of water and drink it. It's as simple as that.

How Much Apple Cider Vinegar Should I Drink Daily?

This is important. Because you don't want to overdo it. That's never a good idea. So how much apple cider vinegar daily? And how much is too much?

Common dosage per day is 15-30 ml. Basically, 1-2 tablespoons of apple cider vinegar – mixed with water or made into a tonic or added to a salad dressing.

My advice is to start with a tablespoon and then increase to 2 tablespoons if you don't notice any side effects. It can be quite strong at first, so you'll want to get used to it.

Potential Side Effects of Drinking Apple Cider Vinegar

Apple cider is rather harmless, but too much of anything can cause problems. Also, there are certain instances when apple cider vinegar is not at all recommended. For example, if you have stomach ulcer or kidney problems.

As a reminder, drinking apple cider vinegar without diluting it is not at all recommended because apple cider vinegar is acidic and it can cause:

- tooth decay and weaken tooth enamel;
- low potassium levels – when drinking more apple cider vinegar than recommended or when you already have low potassium levels;
- indigestion – too much apple cider vinegar can cause indigestion;
- digestive problems – this may sound counterintuitive since apple cider vinegar can improve digestion but for someone who has ulcers or acid reflux, apple cider vinegar will only worsen the symptoms.
- skin burns – another counterintuitive one since apple cider vinegar can soothe sunburn but if you apply it to the skin undiluted it can burn your skin. For treating acne, make sure you add only a little bit of apple cider vinegar in water before applying it to the skin. For sunburn – use 2 tablespoons of apple cider vinegar into your bath water.

CHAPTER 2

Health Benefits of Apple Cider Vinegar, Backed by Science

Apple cider vinegar is a popular home remedy. People have used it for centuries in cooking and medicine.

Many people claim it can relieve a wide range of health complaints, but you may wonder what the research says.

Apple cider vinegar has various healthful properties, including antimicrobial and antioxidant effects. What's more, evidence suggests it may offer health benefits, such as aiding weight loss, reducing cholesterol, lowering blood sugar levels, and improving the symptoms of diabetes.

However, little research exists, and further studies are needed before it can be recommended as an alternative therapy.

This article looks at the evidence behind 6 possible health benefits of apple cider vinegar.

1. High in healthful substances

Apple cider vinegar is made via a two-step process.

First, the manufacturer exposes crushed apples to yeast, which ferments the sugars and turns them into alcohol. Next, they add bacteria to further ferment the alcohol, turning it into acetic acid — the main active compound in vinegar.

Acetic acid gives vinegar its strong sour smell and flavor. Researchers believe this acid is responsible for apple cider vinegar's health benefits. Cider vinegars are 5–6% acetic acid.

Organic, unfiltered apple cider vinegar also contains a substance called mother, which consists of strands of proteins, enzymes, and friendly bacteria that give the product a murky appearance.

Some people believe that the mother is responsible for most of its health benefits, although there are currently no studies to support this.

While apple cider vinegar does not contain many vitamins or minerals, it offers a small amount of potassium. Good quality brands also contain some amino acids and antioxidants.

2. Can help kill harmful bacteria

Vinegar can help kill pathogens, including bacteria.

People have traditionally used vinegar for cleaning and disinfecting, treating nail fungus, lice, warts, and ear infections.

Hippocrates, the father of modern medicine, used vinegar to clean wounds more than 2,000 years ago.

Vinegar is also a food preservative, and studies show that it inhibits bacteria like E. coli from growing in and spoiling food.

If you're looking for a natural way to preserve your food, apple cider vinegar could help.

Anecdotal reports also suggest that diluted apple cider vinegar could help with acne when applied to the skin, but there doesn't seem to be any strong research to confirm this.

3. May help lower blood sugar levels and manage diabetes

To date, one of the most convincing applications of vinegar is helping treat type 2 diabetes.

Type 2 diabetes is characterized by high blood sugar levels caused by insulin resistance or the inability to produce insulin.

However, people without diabetes can also benefit from keeping their blood sugar levels in the normal range, as some researchers believe that high blood sugar levels are a major cause of aging and various chronic diseases.

The most effective and healthiest way to regulate blood sugar levels is to avoid refined carbs and sugar, but apple cider vinegar may also have a beneficial effect.

Research suggests that vinegar offers the following benefits for blood sugar and insulin levels:

- A small study suggests vinegar may improve insulin sensitivity by 19–34% during a high carb meal and significantly lower blood sugar and insulin response.
- In a small study in 5 healthy people, vinegar reduced blood sugar by 31.4% after eating 50 grams of white bread.
- A small study in people with diabetes reported that consuming 2 tablespoons of apple cider vinegar before bedtime reduced fasting blood sugar by 4% the following morning.
- Numerous other studies in humans show that vinegar can improve insulin function and lower blood sugar levels after meals.

The National Centers for Complementary and Integrative Health (NCCIH) says it's very important that people do not replace medical treatment with unproven health products.

If you're currently taking blood-sugar-lowering medications, check with your healthcare provider before increasing your intake of any type of vinegar.

4. May aid weight loss

Perhaps surprisingly, studies show that vinegar could help people lose weight.

Several human studies show that vinegar can increase feelings of fullness. This can lead you to eat fewer calories and lose weight.

For example, according to one study, taking vinegar along with a high carb meal led to increased feelings of fullness, causing participants to eat 200–275 fewer calories throughout the rest of the day.

Furthermore, a study in 175 people with obesity showed that daily apple cider vinegar consumption led to reduced belly fat and weight loss:

- taking 1 tablespoon (12 mL) led to a loss of 2.6 pounds (1.2 kg)
- taking 2 tablespoons (30 mL) led to a loss of 3.7 pounds (1.7 kg)

However, keep in mind that this study went on for 3 months, so the true effects on body weight seem to be rather modest.

That said, simply adding or subtracting single foods or ingredients rarely has a noticeable effect on weight. It's your entire diet or lifestyle that creates long-term weight loss.

Overall, apple cider vinegar may contribute to weight loss by promoting satiety, lowering blood sugar, and reducing insulin levels.

Apple cider vinegar only contains about three calories per tablespoon, which is very low.

5. Improves heart health in animals

Heart disease is one of the leading causes of death.

Several biological factors are linked to your risk of heart disease.

Research suggests that vinegar could improve several of these risk factors. However, many of the studies were conducted in animals.

These animal studies suggest that apple cider vinegar can lower cholesterol and triglyceride levels, as well as several other heart disease risk factors.

Some studies in rats have also shown that vinegar reduces blood pressure, which is a major risk factor for heart disease and kidney problems.

However, there is no good evidence that vinegar benefits heart health in humans. Researchers need to do more studies before reaching any strong conclusions.

6. May boost skin health

Apple cider vinegar is a common remedy for skin conditions like dry skin and eczema.

The skin is naturally slightly acidic. Using topical apple cider vinegar could help rebalance the natural pH of the skin, improving the protective skin barrier.

On the other hand, alkaline soaps and cleansers could irritate eczema, making symptoms worse.

Given its antibacterial properties, apple cider vinegar could, in theory, help prevent skin infections linked to eczema and other skin conditions.

Some people use diluted apple cider vinegar in a facewash or toner. The idea is that it can kill bacteria and prevent spots.

However, one study in 22 people with eczema reported that apple cider vinegar soaks did not improve the skin barrier and caused skin irritation.

Talk to your healthcare provider before trying new remedies, especially on damaged skin. Avoid applying undiluted vinegar to the skin, as it can cause burns.

Dosage and how to use it

The best way to incorporate apple cider vinegar into your diet is to use it in cooking. It's a simple addition to foods like salad dressings and homemade mayonnaise.

Some people also like to dilute it in water and drink it as a beverage. Common dosages range from 1–2 teaspoons (5–10 mL) to 1–2 tablespoon (15–30 mL) per day mixed in a large glass of water.

It's best to start with small doses and avoid taking large amounts. Too much vinegar can cause harmful side effects, including tooth enamel erosion and potential drug interactions.

Some dieticians recommend using organic, unfiltered apple cider vinegars that contain mother."

CHAPTER 3

Apple Cider Vinegar, Cherry and Arthritis

According to the Centers for Disease Control and Prevention (CDC), over 54 million people in the United States report that they've been diagnosed with arthritis. The role of diet in helping to manage arthritis can be confusing. Claims about "miracle" foods seem to be matched by warnings about foods that potentially trigger arthritis symptoms.

Here's a look at how cherry juice and apple cider vinegar may fit into your efforts to tame arthritis pain and stiffness.

The cherry theory

Cherries are a rich source of anthocyanins, which give the fruit its red color. According to the journal Folia Horticulturae, a 100 grams (g) of dark cherries delivers between 82 and 297 milligrams (mg) of anthocyanins.

A member of the flavonoid group, anthocyanins have antioxidant properties that may battle inflammation. However, scientists don't understand exactly how this mechanism works.

Knee pain and tart cherry juice

A double-blind study published in a supplement to the journal Arthritis & Rheumatism revealed that tart cherry juice might have a role in easing pain from osteoarthritis (OA) of the knee.

The study found that people who drank two bottles of tart cherry juice every day for six weeks had decreased pain scores compared with the group that drank a placebo. Each bottle of juice contained the equivalent of 45 tart cherries and a hefty dose of sugar — 31 g.

Popping cherry pills

Researchers have tried to show that cherries can reduce OA pain. One study showed that 20 women with OA had decreased levels of C-reactive protein (CRP) after they drank two bottles of tart cherry juice per day for 21 days. A decreased CRP level is associated with reduced amounts of inflammation.

A study from the Baylor Research Institute showed that a gelatin capsule made from Montmorency cherries could help relieve OA pain. The study was small and wasn't published, and a follow-up study failed to confirm the results. The cherry capsules showed no better pain improvement than placebo in the follow up, according to the Arthritis Foundation.

Cherries and gout

Some research demonstrates a potential role for cherries and cherry extract in reducing gout flares. Gout is a form of arthritis. A gout flare, or "attack," produces joint pain, swelling, and redness.

One study by the Boston University School of Medicine found that eating cherries could help prevent gout attacks. The study followed 633 gout patients for one year. Researchers looked at two-day intervals and found that those who consumed cherries over a two-day period had a 35 percent lower risk of gout attacks than the group that didn't eat cherries at all.

The cherry benefit

The science on a link between cherries and arthritis relief is still evolving. As the research continues, why not enjoy the delicious and healthy red fruit? Here are some ways to get more cherries into your diet:

- Toss dried tart cherries into a salad.
- Stir dried tart cherries into muffin or pancake batter.
- Add a dash of tart cherry juice to your water to give an antioxidant boost to your hydration.
- Top your yogurt and granola with fresh cherries.
- Enjoy a handful of plain fresh cherries.

You can keep your own notes on your arthritis symptoms, and see if cherries help.

The vitals on vinegar

Proponents of apple cider vinegar claim that its antioxidant beta carotene and acetic acid produce miraculous effects in easing arthritis pain. However, no scientific studies support these claims. A United States Department of Agriculture (USDA) analysis of cider vinegar shows no measurable amounts of beta carotene or other vitamins.

A splash of cider vinegar to spark up your salad adds tang but swigging the stuff or swallowing vinegar pills haven't been shown to help arthritis. In fact, the Arthritis Foundation lists apple cider vinegar in an article on arthritis food myths.

Smart use of cherries and apple cider vinegar

No specific "arthritis diet" has been proven to reduce arthritis symptoms. However, a healthy diet is a key part of living well with the condition. Fill your plate with fruit, vegetables, nuts, beans, and seeds to keep weight in check and help control OA.

Healthy eating may also potentially reduce inflammation from gout or rheumatoid arthritis. Include apple cider vinegar and cherries in a fruit- and vegetable-rich diet to help fuel your energy, boost immunity, and stay in a normal weight range.

CHAPTER 4

Apple Cider Vinegar and Diabetes

Type 2 diabetes is a preventable chronic disease that affects how your body controls sugar (glucose) in your blood.

Medications, diet, and exercise are the standard treatments. But recent studies vouch for something you can find in most kitchen cabinets too: apple cider vinegar.

Around 1 in 10 Americans have type 2 diabetes, according to the Centers for Disease Control and Prevention (CDC). If apple cider vinegar has the potential as a natural treatment, that would be good news indeed.

While a number of studies have looked at the link between apple cider vinegar and blood sugar management, they're usually small — with varying results.

"There have been several small studies evaluating the effects of apple cider vinegar, and the results are mixed," said Dr. Maria Peña, an endocrinologist in New York.

"For example, there was one small study done in rats showing that apple cider vinegar helped lower LDL and A1C levels. But the limitation to this study is that it was only done in rats, not humans," she said.

Research from 2004 found that taking 20 grams (equivalent to 20 mL) of apple cider vinegar diluted in 40 mL of water, with 1 teaspoon of saccharine, could lower blood sugar after meals.

Another study, this one from 2007, found that taking apple cider vinegar before bed helped moderate blood sugar upon waking up.

But both studies were small, looking only at 29 and 11 participants, respectively.

Although there's not much research on apple cider vinegar's impact on type 1 diabetes, one small study in 2010 concluded it could help reduce high blood sugar.

A meta-analysis of six studies and 317 patients with type 2 diabetes concludes apple cider vinegar yields beneficial effects on fasting blood sugar and HbA1c.

"The take-home message is that until a large randomized control trial is done, it is difficult to ascertain the true benefits of taking apple cider vinegar," she said.

Still want to try it?

Apple cider vinegar that's organic, unfiltered, and raw is usually the best choice. It may be cloudy and will be higher in beneficial bacteria.

This cloudy cobwebbed chain of acids is called the mother of vinegar culture. It's added to cider or other fluids to start the fermentation of vinegar and is found in high-quality vinegars.

Apple cider vinegar is considered safe, so if you have diabetes, it may be worth trying.

Peña suggests diluting 1 teaspoon of the vinegar in a glass of water to decrease irritation to the stomach and damage to the teeth and cautioned people who are seeking a cure-all.

"People should be wary of any 'quick fix' or 'miracle solution' to their healthcare needs, as these suggestions are not usually backed by strong evidence and can lead to more harm than good," Peña says.

Who should avoid it

According to Peña, people who have kidney problems or ulcers should steer clear, and no one should substitute it for their regular medication.

Large amounts of apple cider vinegar can result in reduced potassium levels in addition to side effects like tooth enamel erosion.

When taking insulin or water pills such as furosemide (Lasix), potassium levels may drop to dangerous levels. Talk to your doctor if you take these medications.

At the end of the day, the most effective way to prevent and manage diabetes is eating a balanced diet that includes healthy carbohydrates and enough healthy proteins and fats.

It's important to understand the impact of carbohydrates on your blood sugar, and limit intake of refined and processed carbohydrates, such as foods with added sugar.

Instead, opt for healthy nutrient-dense, fibrous carbohydrates, such as fruit and vegetables. Contrary to past recommendations, whole grains may also be included in those with kidney disease, as the phosphorus content is now known to be poorly absorbed.

Increasing physical activity can also have a positive impact on blood sugar management.

Peña recommends the research-backed solution of a healthy diet and regular exercise.

Can You Cure Your Acne With Apple Cider Vinegar?

Apple cider vinegar is made by fermenting apple cider, or the unfiltered juice from pressed apples.

It has a variety of uses and has become increasingly popular in the natural health community. It's believed to have many health benefits, including lower blood sugar levels, weight loss and a reduced risk of cancer.

Some even claim it may have benefits for acne, but there is very little research available. This book takes a closer look.

It May Kill Acne-Causing Bacteria

Vinegar is well known for its ability to kill many types of bacteria and viruses.

In fact, it has been shown to reduce the numbers of some bacteria by 90% and certain viruses by 95%.

A type of bacteria known as Propionibacterium acnes, or P. acnes, contributes to the development of acne.

While there isn't much research on the ability of apple cider vinegar to fight P. acnes, there are a few studies on the organic acids it contains.

Apple cider vinegar contains acetic, citric, lactic and succinic acid, all of which have been shown to kill P. acnes.

In one study, 22 people applied lactic acid lotion to their faces twice a day for one year. Most of them experienced a significant reduction in acne, while only two people experienced less than a 50% improvement.

Based on the results of these studies, it's possible that applying apple cider vinegar to your skin can control acne-causing bacteria, but more research is needed.

It May Reduce the Appearance of Scarring

Even after acne heals, it can cause skin discoloration and scarring.

When applied directly to the skin, some of the organic acids found in apple cider vinegar have been shown to help with this.

The process of applying organic acids to the skin is often referred to as "chemical peeling." The acids remove the damaged, outer layers of the skin and promote regeneration.

Specifically, chemical peeling with succinic acid has been shown to suppress inflammation caused by P. acnes, which may help prevent scarring.

Lactic acid has also been shown to improve the texture, pigmentation and appearance of the skin in individuals with superficial acne scars.

While studies on organic acids show promising results, more studies are needed to explore the effects of apple cider vinegar on scarring.

Applying It to Your Skin Can Cause Burns

Apple cider vinegar is strongly acidic by nature. Because of this, it may cause burns when applied directly to the skin.

In most cases, burns occur after apple cider vinegar has been in contact with the skin for long periods of time.

Shorter periods of skin contact are less likely to cause burns.

In order to prevent skin damage, apple cider vinegar should be used in small amounts and diluted with water.

You should also avoid using apple cider vinegar on sensitive skin and open wounds, as it's more likely to cause pain or skin damage in those cases.

If you apply apple cider vinegar to your skin and feel a burning sensation, try diluting it with more water. If it still burns, you may want to stop using it.

Should You Use Apple Cider Vinegar to Treat Acne?

Apple cider vinegar contains organic acids that may help kill the bacteria that cause acne.

It may also help reduce the appearance of scars.

However, studies on this are inconclusive, and some cases of severe acne require a more rigorous treatment plan.

Furthermore, applying apple cider vinegar directly to the skin can cause skin damage and burns, especially for those with sensitive skin or open wounds.

Because of this, it may cause more harm than good in individuals with acne.

How to Treat Acne with Apple Cider Vinegar

Due to its high acidity, apple cider vinegar should be diluted before it's applied to the skin. Here are some simple steps you can follow:

1. Mix 1 part apple cider vinegar with 3 three parts water (if you have sensitive skin, you may want to use more water).
2. Cleanse your face with mild face wash and pat dry.
3. Using a cotton ball, gently apply the mixture to the affected skin.
4. Let sit for 5–20 seconds, rinse with water and pat dry.
5. Repeat this process 1–2 times per day.

Additionally, use organic apple cider vinegar that contains "the mother." This is the cloudy substance that typically sinks to the bottom of the bottle.

It contains proteins, enzymes and beneficial bacteria that are responsible for most of apple cider vinegar's health benefits.

For this reason, apple cider vinegar with "the mother" may provide more benefits than the filtered and refined varieties.

The organic acids in apple cider vinegar may help kill the bacteria that cause acne.

They may also help reduce the appearance of scars.

However, the few studies that exist on this topic are inconclusive, and apple cider vinegar might not work for everyone.

CHAPTER 5

The Health Benefits of Apple Cider Vinegar

Apple cider vinegar is a liquid produced during the fermentation of apple cider. During this process, the sugar in apples is fermented by yeast and/or bacteria added to the cider, which then turns it into alcohol and, finally, into vinegar.

Like other types of vinegar, the key component in apple cider vinegar is acetic acid. Apple cider vinegar also contains other substances such as lactic, citric, and malic acids, and bacteria.

For centuries, apple cider vinegar has been used as a home remedy to treat many health ailments and as a disinfectant and natural preservative.

Health Benefits

Proponents claim that apple cider vinegar may boost your health in a variety of ways. Science backs up some of these claims.

Blood Sugar

The acetic acid in vinegar appears to block enzymes that help you digest starch, resulting in a smaller blood sugar response after starchy meals such as pasta or bread.

A 2017 review of studies published in Diabetes Research & Clinical Practice suggested that the increased intake of vinegar with meals can decrease fluctuations in insulin and blood sugar after meals.

To incorporate apple cider vinegar in your meals, try adding a splash to salads, marinades, vinaigrettes, and sauces. If you have diabetes or prediabetes, be sure to consult your doctor if you're considering using amounts larger than those normally found in cooking. Vinegar can interact with diabetes medication, and it shouldn't be used by people with certain health conditions, like gastroparesis.

Weight Loss

Proponents claim that consuming vinegar before or with a meal may have a satiating effect. A 12-week study from Japan reported that people who had consumed up to 30 milliliters (roughly 6 teaspoons) of vinegar per day experienced a modest one-to-two pound reduction in body weight. Body mass index (BMI), waist circumference, triglycerides, and visceral fat were also slightly reduced.

People tend to consume greater than normal amounts of apple cider vinegar when using it for weight loss purposes, with some even taking it in tablet form.

Other Uses

Over the years, apple cider vinegar has been used as a home remedy for many health and beauty issues. While there isn't strong science to back these claims, there is some anecdotal evidence to affirm its potential.

Dandruff

To address dandruff, some people find that lightly spritzing an apple cider vinegar and water solution onto the scalp combats persistent flakes, itchiness, and irritation. Vinegar's acetic acid may alter the scalp's pH, making it harder for yeast—one of the main contributors to dandruff—to flourish. It has also been suggested that it can treat a form of eczema known as seborrheic dermatitis.

A 2017 study published in the Galen Medical Journal suggested that the topical application of the flowering herb Althaea officinalis combined with vinegar was able to resolve seborrheic dermatitis is a 32-year-old woman.

Although apple cider vinegar is sometimes recommended as a hair rinse to remove shampoo build-up and clarify dull hair, the solution has to be very dilute in order to prevent stinging the eyes.

Sunburn and Other Skin Injuries

While the more common recommendation for a mild sunburn is a cool water compress, cool bath, aloe gel, or moisturizer, some people swear by apple cider vinegar. It can be added to a cool bath or mixed with cool water and lightly spritzed on affected areas (avoiding the face) to relieve pain and discomfort.

There is little evidence that apple cider vinegar can help heal or relieve sunburn pain better than no treatment. It does, however, have excellent antibacterial properties that may help prevent skin infections caused by sunburn and other skin injuries.

Apple cider vinegar shouldn't be applied full-strength or in strong concentrations to the skin, as the acidity can further injure the skin. It also shouldn't be used for more serious burns. Be sure to consult your health care provider for help in determining the severity of your sunburn.

If you have mosquito bites, poison ivy, or jellyfish stings, a weak apple cider vinegar solution dabbed onto bites and stings may help itching and irritation.

Acne and Other Chronic Skin Disorders

Apple cider vinegar may help to dry out pimples when a solution is dabbed onto pimples. It should be diluted before applying it to the face as it can cause skin injury or chemical burns if it's not dilute enough.

The concentration of acetic acid in apple cider vinegar varies widely and is not standardized, making it difficult to judge how much to dilute it to be safe as a skin toner or for other purposes.

Although the evidence supporting the use of apple cider vinegar in treating acne is lacking, research has suggested that it may help diminish the appearance of varicose veins when applied topically.

Sore Throat

A time-honored throat elixir, apple cider vinegar drinks, and gargles are said to alleviate the pain of a sore throat (pharyngitis). Although there are many different recipes and protocols, a basic drink recipe calls for a teaspoon of apple cider vinegar, a teaspoon of honey, and a small pinch of cayenne pepper stirred in a cup of warm water.

Although proponents claim that apple cider vinegar has germ-fighting properties and capsaicin in hot peppers alleviates pain, there hasn't been any research on apple cider vinegar's ability to fight sore throats. Moreover, there is evidence that treating a sore throat with vinegar can cause more harm than good.

If not properly diluted, vinegar can corrode esophageal tissues, causing persistent throat pain and dysphagia (difficulty swallowing).

It is unclear at what concentration apple cider vinegar would safe for use in treating pharyngitis, particularly in children.

Deodorant

To help keep smelly feet under control, proponents claim apple cider vinegar may help to balance the skin's pH and fight the bacteria that causes foot odor. Typically, a bit of apple cider vinegar is mixed into water. Baby wipes, cotton balls or pads, small towels, or cotton rags can be dipped into the solution, wrung out, and used to wipe the bottom of the feet. Wipes can be made ahead and stored in an airtight container.

Although a vinegar scent will be noticeable, it often dissipates when the vinegar solution has dried. Avoid wearing shoes made from materials like leather that can be damaged by the acidity.

An apple cider vinegar solution can also help to neutralize odor-causing armpit bacteria. Typically, cotton pads, towelettes, or cotton rags are lightly spritzed with a very weak solution and swiped onto the armpits. The vinegar smell should dissipate as it dries.

It's a good idea to test the apple cider vinegar solution in a smaller area first and to avoid using it if you're wearing delicate fibers, like silk.

Possible Side Effects

Apple cider vinegar is a popular household ingredient, which may lead you to believe that it's completely safe. While there may be no cause for alarm if you are generally healthy, there are some potential effects to be aware of, particularly if the concentration is too strong or is in contact with your body for too long.

Apple cider vinegar, for instance, may cause chemical burns. There have been case reports of chemical burns after apple cider vinegar was used for warts and a skin condition known as molluscum contagiosum.

Although apple cider vinegar is widely touted as a home remedy to whiten teeth or freshen breath, exposing your teeth to the acidity may erode tooth enamel and lead to cavities.

When taken internally, ACV may result in decreased potassium levels, hypoglycemia, throat irritation, and allergic reactions. It is an acid (a pH less than 7 is an acid, and many apple cider vinegar products have a pH of 2 to 3) and can cause burns and injury to the digestive tract (including the throat, esophagus, and stomach), especially when taken undiluted or in large amounts.

Apple cider vinegar may interact with certain medications, including laxatives, diuretics, blood thinners, and heart disease and diabetes medications.

Apple cider vinegar shouldn't be used as a nasal spray, sinus wash, or in a neti pot, and it shouldn't be added to eye drops. Vinegar won't help in the treatment of lice.

Dosage and Preparation

Apple cider vinegar is available as a liquid and in supplement capsules. There is no standard dose for ACV supplements, so follow the package directions and check with your healthcare provider.

When using vinegar, most suggested uses involve diluting apple cider vinegar before applying it to the body. However, the safety of different vinegar-to-water ratios isn't known. A 1:10 ratio has been suggested when applying it directly to skin, however, it should be weaker (or avoided entirely) on weak or delicate skin.

Although a teaspoon to a tablespoon mixed into 8 ounces of water is often suggested as a reasonable amount for internal use, the safety of various doses isn't known.

You can try to use it highly diluted, but the amount of acetic acid in commercial apple cider vinegar varies (unlike white vinegar, which is 5% acetic acid) making it impossible to be sure of the true strength.

What to Look For

Apple cider vinegar is available filtered or unfiltered. Filtered apple cider is a clear light brown color. Unfiltered and unpasteurized ACV (such as Bragg's apple cider vinegar) has dark, cloudy sediment at the bottom of the bottle. Known as "mother of vinegar" or simply "the mother," this sediment consists mainly of acetic acid bacteria. Apple cider vinegar is also available in tablet form.

When buying apple cider vinegar in supplement form, read the product label to ensure that apple cider vinegar is listed in the ingredients rather than acetic acid (white vinegar).

CHAPTER 6

30 Surprising Uses for Apple Cider Vinegar

Interestingly, it also has a ton of different beauty, household and cooking uses.

Apple cider vinegar uses include cleaning, washing hair, preserving food and improving skin function.

It can also be used in all sorts of recipes, including salad dressings, soups, sauces, hot drinks and more.

Here are 30 ways to use apple cider vinegar.

1. To Lower Blood Sugar

Apple cider vinegar is claimed to help diabetics control their blood sugar levels.

Some studies have shown that consuming vinegar after a high-carb meal can improve insulin sensitivity by as much as 34% and reduce blood sugar levels significantly.

However, if you're on medication for diabetes, you should check with your doctor before taking apple cider vinegar.

2. To Help You Feel Full

Apple cider vinegar is sometimes recommended as a weight loss aid.

This is because it may help you feel full.

Some short-term studies have shown that consuming apple cider vinegar may help you eat fewer calories, lose weight and reduce belly fat.

However, its long-term effects on weight loss are unknown and likely to be small unless other dietary and lifestyle changes are also made.

3. To Preserve Food

Just like other types of vinegar, apple cider vinegar is an effective preservative.

In fact, people have used vinegar as a pickling agent to preserve foods for thousands of years.

It works by making the food more acidic, which deactivates its enzymes and kills any bacteria in the food that may cause spoilage.

4. As a Deodorizer

Apple cider vinegar is known to have antibacterial properties.

Because of this, it's often claimed that apple cider vinegar can eliminate bad smells.

There isn't any research to back up these claims, but you can try it out by mixing apple cider vinegar with water to make a deodorizing spray.

This makes a natural alternative to odor neutralizers.

You can also mix it with water and Epsom salts to make a foot soak.

This may help get rid of unwanted foot odor by killing off odor-causing bacteria.

5. To Make a Salad Vinaigrette

One easy way to use apple cider vinegar is to make a simple salad dressing.

Homemade salad dressings can be much healthier for you than store-bought ones, and they're often tastier too.

6. To Lower the Risk of Cancer

It's often claimed that apple cider vinegar can help lower your risk of cancer.

In test-tube studies, vinegar has been shown to kill cancer cells.

Some observational studies, which can't prove causation, have also linked consuming apple cider vinegar with a decreased risk of esophageal cancer. However, other studies have linked it with an increased risk of bladder cancer.

Overall, there is insufficient evidence to make any claims regarding the effects of apple cider vinegar on the risk of cancer.

7. To Make an All-Purpose Cleaner

Apple cider vinegar is often a popular choice for a natural alternative to commercial cleaning agents. This is because of its antibacterial properties.

Mix 1 cup of water with half a cup of apple cider vinegar, and you'll have a natural all-purpose cleaner.

However, it's worth noting that although vinegars such as apple cider vinegar can kill some bacteria, they aren't as effective at killing harmful bacteria as commercial cleaning agents.

8. To Soothe a Sore Throat

Apple cider vinegar is a popular home remedy for sore throats.

It's thought that its antibacterial properties could help kill off the bacteria that could be causing the problem. However, there is no evidence to support its use in this way.

If you try this at home, make sure you mix the vinegar with water before gargling.

This is because apple cider vinegar is very acidic and has been known to cause throat burns when consumed undiluted.

9. As a Facial Toner

Anecdotally, apple cider vinegar is claimed to help remedy skin conditions and reduce the signs of aging.

As such, many people like to use apple cider vinegar to make a skin tonic.

The general recipe is 1 part apple cider vinegar to 2 parts water. This is then applied to the skin using a cotton pad. However, if you have sensitive skin, you may want to make a more diluted solution.

10. To Trap Fruit Flies

Fruit flies can be a pest.

Interestingly, it's really easy to use apple cider vinegar to make a cheap fruit fly trap.

Simply pour some apple cider vinegar into a cup, add a few drops of dish soap (so that any trapped flies sink) and you're good to go.

11. To Boil Better Eggs

Adding vinegar to the water you use to boil or poach eggs can help you produce consistently good eggs.

This is because the protein in egg whites firm up more quickly when exposed to a more acidic liquid.

When you're poaching eggs, you want the egg whites to firm up as quickly as possible so that the eggs keep their shape.

Using vinegar when boiling eggs can also speed up the coagulation, or clotting, of the egg whites. This can be useful if the shell cracks while the egg is being boiled.

12. As a Marinade

Another way to use apple cider vinegar when cooking is to make a marinade.

In fact, apple cider vinegar is a popular ingredient in many steak marinades, as it gives the meat a nice sweet and sour flavor.

Combine it with wine, garlic, soy sauce, onion and cayenne pepper to give your steak a delicious flavor.

13. To Wash Fruits and Vegetables

Pesticide residue on fruits and vegetables can be a concern for many people.

That's why some people like to wash their fruits and vegetables in apple cider vinegar. The hope is that it'll remove more of the chemical residues than water alone.

Although it's not entirely clear if it will remove more pesticides than simply washing with water, it may help kill any dangerous bacteria on food.

For example, washing foods in vinegar has been shown to remove dangerous bacteria like E. coli and Salmonella.

14. To Clean Dentures

You can also use apple cider vinegar to clean dentures.

Although there's no consensus on the best method to clean dentures, it's thought that the residues left by apple cider vinegar could be less harmful to the skin in your mouth than other cleaning agents.

15. In the Bath

For the same reasons people like using apple cider vinegar as a homemade facial toner, they also like using it in the bath.

If you want to try it, add 1–2 cups of apple cider vinegar to your bath water and enjoy a soak in your tub.

16. As a Hair Rinse

An apple cider vinegar hair rinse is said to remove product buildup, detangle and add shine to your hair.

Try mixing 1 part apple cider vinegar with 1 part water and pour the mixture over your hair. Leave it in for a few minutes before washing it out.

If you have sensitive skin, then you should try doing this with a weaker dilution first, as the vinegar is quite acidic.

17. As a Dandruff Treatment

Massaging diluted apple cider vinegar into your scalp may help get rid of dandruff.

It's unclear how effective this is, but the theory is that the acid in the vinegar could help stop the growth of the fungus Malassezia, which may contribute to dandruff.

18. In a Sauce

Apple cider vinegar can be a great ingredient for a tangy sauce for your food. Try adding it to tomato-based sauces to give them a fuller flavor.

19. In Soup

Adding vinegar to soup can help bring its flavors to life.

If your favorite homemade soup tastes a little bland, try adding a little vinegar to it at the end. Add it gradually until the soup tastes great.

20. As a Weed Killer

Another great use for apple cider vinegar is as a homemade weed killer.

Spray undiluted vinegar on unwanted weeds in your garden to get rid of them. You can also try mixing it with soap and lemon juice to see if that makes it more effective.

21. In Homemade Cakes and Candies

Apple cider vinegar is a popular flavor and texture enhancer in baking, especially when making vegan treats that can't include eggs.

It can also add extra flavor to homemade candy and caramels.

22. In a Hot Drink

Mix 2 tablespoons of apple cider vinegar, 1 teaspoon of cinnamon, 1 tablespoon of honey and 2 tablespoons of lemon juice into 12 oz (355 ml) of hot water for an alternative hot drink.

23. As a Mouth Wash

Apple cider vinegar is often said to be a useful alternative to commercial mouthwashes.

Its antibacterial properties may help with bad breath, although there aren't any studies examining how effective it is.

If you try this, make sure you dilute it well with water (the usual amount is 1 tablespoon for every cup, or 240 ml, of water), as the acidity of the vinegar could damage your teeth.

24. To Clean Your Tooth Brush

To have really clean teeth, it's worth considering how clean your toothbrush is.

Given that apple cider vinegar has antibacterial properties, you can use it as a homemade cleaner for your toothbrush.

To make your own toothbrush cleaner, mix half a cup (120 ml) of water with 2 tablespoons (30 ml) of apple cider vinegar and 2 teaspoons of baking soda and mix well.

Leave the head of your toothbrush in the mix for 30 minutes.

Make sure you rinse your brush well before you use it, as the acidity of undiluted vinegar could damage your teeth.

25. To Whiten Teeth

Apple cider vinegar is acidic, so some people like to use it to remove stains and whiten their teeth.

To try this, rub a small amount of apple cider vinegar onto your teeth with a cotton swab. The results aren't instant, but repeated use could remove stains over time.

However, be wary of this method for teeth whitening. Be sure to rinse out your mouth really well afterward, as the acid can damage the enamel on your teeth.

26. To Treat Acne

Dabbing small amounts of diluted apple cider vinegar onto pimples is claimed to be a good way to get rid of them.

However, undiluted apple cider vinegar is strongly acidic and putting it directly onto your skin can cause burns.

27. To Get Rid of Warts

As with acne, apple cider vinegar is claimed to be a natural agent for getting rid of warts. It's likely effective for removing warts from skin due to its acidic nature.

However, be aware that this method is very painful, and some people who've tried it has required a local anesthetic.

28. As a Natural Deodorant

Wiping your underarms with diluted apple cider vinegar is said to be a homemade alternative to commercially produced deodorants.

That said, although it's popular in some circles, it's not clear how effective it is.

29. As a Dish Detergent

Rinsing your dishes in apple cider vinegar could help kill off any unwanted bacteria and keep them clean.

Some people add it to their dishwater, while others even put it in their dishwasher.

30. To Get Rid of Fleas

Apple cider vinegar may help prevent your pet from getting fleas.

It's thought that spraying a mixture of 1 part water and 1 part apple cider vinegar onto your pet will create an environment that fleas won't want to hang around in.

Apple cider vinegar is an extremely versatile household item that has a ton of different uses.

It can be a cheap and easy way to tackle many problems around your home.

Other Uses for Apple Cider Vinegar

Apple cider vinegar, the amazing magical elixir. What can't it do?

Women use apple cider vinegar for just about everything, from the expected (salad dressing) to the... surprising (cleaning the Mooncup). It's like the Swiss Army knife of a real food kitchen.

But just how versatile is apple cider vinegar?

Apple cider vinegar is something the mamas in my community talk about all the time.

But just how many uses are there for apple cider vinegar?

Apple Cider Vinegar for Skincare

1. Eczema remedy

I dab ACV on my little one's eczema.

2. Skin toner

I use equal parts water and ACV for a skin toner.

3. Natural astringent for acne

Mix 1 part water 1 part cider vinegar dip cotton ball apply to face until dry then rinse.

4. Facial mask

I'm about to mix it with some green clay.

5. Mole remover

Dip a piece of cotton (I use a small piece if a cotton pad) in ACV, ring out a bit then place it on your wart, skin tag or mole, then place a bandaid over it. I like to leave it on over night.

6. Wart remover

Soak a cotton ball in ACV, place over wart and cover with medical tape. Repeat daily till the nasty thing vanishes.

7. Facial wash

Simply mix 1 part ACV and 2 parts water and rub on your face. Add some raw honey to the mixture if your skin is dry. Then rinse with warm water.

8. Make up remover

Mix 1 part ACV and 2 parts water. Dab a cotton ball with the mixture and swipe on makeup to remove.

9. Soften skin

We even soak in it for our skin is so soft afterwards.

10. Sunburn

Soak washcloth and place on sunburn. Takes the sting out and reduces the redness.

11. Healing all sorts of skin issues

12. Skin tags

Dip a piece of cotton (I use a small piece if a cotton pad) in ACV, ring out a bit then place it on your skin tag then place a bandaid over it. I like to leave it on over night.

Apple Cider Vinegar for Cleaning

13. Fabric Softener

I use 1 cup of ACV.

14. Cleaner

Cleaning: Spray on surfaces, or pour on scrubby...add baking soda, scrub away. Pour down garbage disposal w/baking soda and a lemon. Let sit for a few minutes, then turn on the water and the disposal.

15. Rinsing agent in washing machine

Add one cup of ACV to the rinse cycle.

16. Cleaning the mooncup

Wash your menstrual cup in a 50/50 ACV and water mixture with some gentle soap.

17. Keep ants away

Ants avoid that stuff like its poison, just pour.

18. Fruitfly trap / fly trap / gnat

In a bowl with plastic wrap on top tightly. Poke holes with tooth pick to catch flies.

19. Cleans humidifier

Remove the filter and rinse with water. Then add ACV to the tank of the humidifier and let sit for 30 minutes, swishing around occasionally. Rinse and dry.

20. Drain cleaner

Acv and baking soda to clear a clogged drain.

21. Whiten laundry

I also put 1/4 cup in with my white laundry and baking soda to brighten it up.

22. Jewelry cleaner

Mix 1/2 cup ACV and 2 tbsp. baking soda and let silver jewelry sit in the mixture for a few hours. Rinse with clean water and dry and shine with a soft cloth.

23. Weed killer

Just pour ACV on the weeds!

24. Cleaning menstrual sponges

Wash your menstrual sponge in a 50/50 ACV and water mixture with some gentle soap.

25. For cloth diapers

Add 1/2 cup to the first rinse of a load of cloth diapers.

Apple Cider Vinegar for Pets

26. Keep away cats

The cats aren't fans, so we use it to keep them away from places they shouldn't be!

27. Flea spray

Spray a 50/50 mixtures of ACV and water on your pet before they go outside.

28. Ward off parasites

I put a capful in my dogs water bowl.

29. Conjunctivitis of dogs

Mix 1 part ACV and 2 parts water. Dab a cloth in the mixture and apply BELOW the eyes. reapply every few hours.

30. Ear mites in cats and dogs

50/50 acv and water rinse 2 times a day for 2 weeks. works like magic, and no trip to the vet!

31. Homemade dog shampoo

Mix 1 part ACV, 1 part water, and 1 part baby shampoo (not Castile soap).

32. Chicken immune system booster

Put 1 tbsp per gallon to boosts my chickens immune system.

Apple Cider Vinegar for Wellness

33. Helps slow the breakdown of carbohydrates

Also add 1tbls to each serving of pasta.

34. Arthritis

I drink 2 tsp in 8 oz of water to help relieve my arthritis symptoms.

35. For weight loss

I love drinking a tablespoon in a glass of water! It quenches your thirst so much better than just water.

36. Help blood glucose levels

I drink it in water all day.

37. Prevent mastitis

Drink it in water on a daily basis.

38. Regulate PCOS symptoms

I drink about a tbsp in 8 oz of water before meals.

39. PMS Symptoms/cramps

Helps with PMS symptoms, mostly cramps.

Add a teaspoon of ACV to a cup of water 3 times a day.

40. Lowers cholesterol

Add a teaspoon of ACV to a cup of water 3 times a day.

41. PH balance

Can help regulate your body's pH which can ward off disease. Consume 1 teaspoon mixed in a cup of water daily.

42. Immune system building / booster tea

Warm water, ACV, cinnamon & honey. Tastes like hot apple cider.

43. Tea/tonic/drinks

Drink 2 tbs. of ACV, 1 tbs. of raw local honey, 1 tsp. of cinnamon, and half a lemon to 1 cup of water.

44. Energy drink

A teaspoon to a tablespoon of ACV in 8 ounces of water. With a tablespoon or so of raw honey, a splash of lemon juice, and a dash of ground ginger. Mix it all up and drink before every meal.

Apple Cider Vinegar for Beauty

45. For dry scalp / dandruff treatment

Add ACV to your shampoo before washing.

46. Hair rinse / hair wash / hair soak

I usually do about a cap full of it into a water bottle along with filling the bottle up to half with warm water and leaving it in my hair for a few minutes then rinse out.

47. Cellulite cleanser

ACV helps break down fat in cells. Add a teaspoon of ACV to a cup of water every day.

48. Gargle

Use a 50/50 ACV and water mixture to gargle with.

49. Hair conditioner / detangler / hair spray

I dilute it with water and use it as conditioner.

50. Teeth whitener

Brush your teeth with ACV before you brush with regular toothpaste.

51. Grow in balding spots of hair / helps fix alopacea

Add a teaspoon of ACV to a cup of water every day.

52. Soften hair

Use a 50/50 mix of ACV and water as a hair rinse.

53. Bath soak / detox bath

I use it in the bath as a detoxifying soak along with epsom salts and coconut oil, really helps with skin issues.

54. Set hair dye.

Dilute with water and rinse after dying, rinsing and conditioning.

Apple Cider Vinegar for Natural Remedies

55. Heartburn / fighting pregnancy induced heartburn

I mix a tablespoon of acv with a glass of freshly pressed apple juice and drink.

56. For sore throats, coughs, lost voices

Hot water, 2 tbsps cider vinegar, 2 tbsps honey.

57. Indigestion / upset stomach

I throw a tablespoon of ACV into my water every day to give it some flavor.

58. Fungus-like ring worm / kill toenail fungus

Soak feet every day in it.

59. Kill candida

Ingest a tablespoon mixed with water daily to rid body of candida overgrowth.

60. Dermatitis

Use it on contact dermatitis.

61. Aches and pains (especially joint pain)

Consume 1 teaspoon mixed in a cup of water daily.

62. Plantar wart removal

Soak for 10 mins each night before bed until gone.

63. Morning sickness

I put a teaspoon or so in a glass of water with a little stevia. It neutralizes the acid in the stomach!

64. Acid reflux/GERD

I add one tablespoon to a glass of water and drink for immediate relief of acid reflux pain.

65. Cold / sick / fever remedy

Mixed in with honey, lemon, cinnamon, (sometimes garlic) for a cold remedy.

66. Diaper rashes

Put it in the bath for diaper rashes.

67. Clear sinuses

Boil it with water and inhale to clear sinuses.

68. Foot soak / for athlete's foot/ foot scrub

1 part ACV to 4 parts water.

69. UTI's.

In a bath for UTI's. Add a cup or two of ACV to your bath.

70. Strep B tests

Consume 1 teaspoon mixed in a cup of water daily.

71. Thrush

Water and ACV mixture swabbed onto my nipples after breastfeeding during a thrush in babies situation.

72. Stop a gallbladder attack

A tablespoon before every meal keeps me from having gallbladder attacks.

1 T acv + 1 cup apple juice = stops gallbladder attacks.

1/4 C for gallbladder attacks.

I would drink a mix of half ACV and half water or better, apple juice.

73. Deodorant

I splash a little on my underarms before I use my homemade deodorant. Otherwise, the baking soda in it makes me itch. The acv balances out the pH.

74. Nausea / vomiting / diarrhea

Equal parts ACV and raw honey, enough water to drink it down.

75. Muscle cramps

A shot helps with muscle cramps.

76. Bursitis

My doctor has me drink two tablespoons in warm water to treat my bursitis.

77. Natural antihistamine

Consume 1 teaspoon mixed in a cup of water daily.

78. Cures molloscum

Either taken internally or place on warts with cotton ball and bandaid for an hour.

79. Fever blister remedy

I put it straight on a few times a day.

80. Yeast infection

Mix in douche bottle 1/4 bragg's raw ACV with 3/4 lukewarm water. 2x per day for 3 days.

Pour one cup into a bath.

81. Cradle cap

Apply to a baby's head to kill the bacteria that causes cradle cap.

82. Soak new clothes in it to set color

83. Shrink my fibroid

Consume 1-2 teaspoon mixed in a cup of water daily.

84. Earache

Few drops in the ear for an earache.

85. Cellulitis

Consume 1-2 teaspoon mixed in a cup of water daily.

86. For respiratory problems

It is wonderful for respiratory problems (cold, asthma, bronchitis, allergy, etc) used in a humidifier 4:1 with distilled water.

Food & cooking

87. In bone broth

Add 2 tablespoons to your homemade bone broth.

88. For washing fruits and veggies/wash produce

I also have it in a spray bottle diluted with water for cleaning, especially veggies.

89. Make buttermilk

Add 1 Tbsp. apple cider vinegar to 1 cup of milk. Allow to sit at room temperature until the milk thickens.

90. Salad dressing

With EVOO, lime and pinch of salt as a my every day salad dressing.

91. Pickle bologna

92. Soaking grains

Add 1-2 tbsp to your soaking grains.

93. Cooking

94. Vinaigrette

95. Homemade mayonaise

96. Buttermilk pancakes

Add to milk to make "buttermilk" pancakes.

Add 1 T ACV to dairy free milk (soy, almond, etc) and let sit to curdle. Makes vegan/dairy free "buttermilk" for baking!

97. Baking

Add ACV and baking soda to get baked goods to rise better.

98. Roast

I add it to my roast so it's juicy.

99. Chutney

Add some ACV while cooking Chutney to soften the fruit.

100. Hard boiled eggs

Add some ACV to the water when boiling eggs to help avoid broken shells.

101. Marinade

Use ACV in your marinade recipe to help tenderize the meat and add a richer flavor.

CHAPTER 7

Ways to Use Apple Cider Vinegar- Explained

Apple cider vinegar with mother is a fermented juice made from crushed apples. Apple cider vinegar is a popular ingredient in many detoxifying and cleansing recipes because it contains so many vitamins, minerals and antioxidants. Some nutrients in apple cider vinegar include acetic and folic acids, and minerals, such as potassium, iron and magnesium. Apple cider vinegar also contains polyphenols, which are powerful antioxidants.

Apple cider vinegar is a classic home remedy. There are many home remedies and historical apple cider vinegar uses, ranging from soothing a throat to supporting skin and hair health. Additionally, apple cider vinegar has been highlighted in studies that show it may have benefits for weight management with diet and exercise, blood sugar health that is in the normal range and heart health.

The benefits of apple cider vinegar (ACV) are definitely no secret. Use of this popular kitchen staple dates to ancient times, and it may have been used by Hippocrates himself.[1] While times (and apple cider vinegar uses) have changed a lot since then, ACV is still a versatile, well-known ingredient kept in many homes.

There are tons of ways to incorporate apple cider vinegar into your daily routine, as you'll see below. One of the most popular ways to add this amazing, whole-body health tonic to your diet is by making drinks with apple cider vinegar. For example, check out this easy recipe for a detox drink using Swanson's Apple Cider Vinegar, or look below for the perfect drink recipe for new users of apple cider vinegar.

Before we get into ACV recipes, it's important to discuss when to drink apple cider vinegar. The best way to maximize the health benefits of apple cider vinegar is to drink it on an empty stomach.

Dilute it with a bit of water and drink it about 20 minutes before you eat your regular meal, otherwise the foods you eat can actually make the apple cider vinegar less potent. Also, apple cider vinegar can help when you know you're going to be eating foods that usually don't agree with you. Tip: mix apple cider vinegar with honey to soothe your stomach.

Here are some creative ways to add the benefits of apple cider vinegar to your life.

Uses for Apple Cider Vinegar

While the uses for white vinegar are vast and well known, apple cider vinegar may actually be the more versatile and more beneficial of the two. And no, white vinegar and apple cider vinegar are not the same things, so read your labels carefully.

There are questions asked all the time, "what is apple cider vinegar good for?" The answer, as you'll see, depends on how you want to use it, where you want to use and for what reason you may need to use it. From the kitchen to the bathroom to your medicine cabinet, apple cider vinegar can be used in often surprising ways. Let's take a look.

1. Apple Cider Vinegar Salad Dressing: Use apple cider vinegar in homemade salad dressings instead of balsamic vinegar.

2. Apple Cider Vinegar Smoothie: Add to 2 tablespoons to your morning smoothie for an extra energy kick but be careful — it has a pretty strong taste, so just add a little at a time.

3. Apple Cider Vinegar Facial Toner: Mix 1 part apple cider vinegar and 3 to 4 parts water and use as a facial toner.2 Apply to skin with a cotton pad, let it sit for about 10 minutes, then rinse. Repeat three times a day.

4. Apple Cider Vinegar Digestive Tonic: Mix 2 teaspoons apple cider vinegar with 1 tablespoon each of fresh ginger, water and fresh lemon juice. Add 8 ounces of sparkling water, then add raw honey to taste. Pour over ice and enjoy! (Ginger is also well-known for its stomach-soothing properties.

5. All-Purpose Cleaner with Apple Cider Vinegar: Mix apple cider vinegar in equal parts with water, then add a few drops of essential oil, like lemon oil, for an all-purpose cleaner.

6. Boost Bone Broth: Boost your homemade bone broth by adding 2 tablespoons after you're done cooking the bone broth.

7. Apple Cider Vinegar Detox Bath: Add 1 cup apple cider vinegar, 2 cups Epsom salts and a few drops of lavender essential oil to bathwater for a relaxing and detoxifying bath.

8. Apple Cider Vinegar Body Scrub: A 2 tablespoons of apple cider vinegar to 1 cup of granulated sugar and 1 tablespoon of honey for a whole-body scrub.

9. Trap Fruit Flies: Pour a thin layer of apple cider vinegar into a cup and add a drop of dish soap. Set it out on the counter and the fruit flies will fly in and get stuck.

10. Remove Cat Urine: If your cat has an accident, add apple cider vinegar to your laundry when you wash the item to help remove the smell.

11. Banish Bad Breath: Mix 1/2 tablespoon with 1 cup of water and gargle 10 seconds, spit and repeat to banish bad breath.

12. Post-Workout Recovery: Fight lactic acid buildup by adding 1 tablespoon to your bottle of water after a workout.

13. Apple Cider Vinegar Hair Treatment: Briefly soak your hair with 1/3 cup of apple cider vinegar after shampooing then rinse for shiny, detangled hair.

14. Whiten Teeth: Apple cider vinegar can help spruce up your pearly-whites by using it as a gargle after brushing to help remove stains.

15. Apple Cider Vinegar Throat Soother: Combine in equal parts with water to make a throat-soothing gargle that you can use hourly.

16. Apple Cider Vinegar as a Dairy Free Buttermilk Substitute: Use apple cider vinegar to make a quick buttermilk substitute by adding 1 tablespoon to 1 cup of milk and letting the mixture sit until it thickens. Or, make a homemade buttermilk substitute by using apple cider vinegar to sour rice milk, following the same 1 tablespoon to 1 cup ratio. Use it to make yummy recipes like cornbread or biscuits.

17. Apple Cider Vinegar Liver Detox Tonic: Mix with pure, sparkling water (about 8 ounces) for a DIY liver tonic. "It's very refreshing and good for the liver."

18. Apple Cider Vinegar Metabolism Boost: Enhance fat burn during workouts by adding 1 tablespoon of apple cider vinegar to your water bottle.

19. Remove Hair Product Buildup: Apply apple cider vinegar (about 1 to 3 tablespoons) to your scalp in the shower to clean and remove buildup.

20. Healthy Apple Cider Vinegar Marinade: Use it to marinate steaks for about 30 minutes before grilling to enhance flavor.

21. Apple Cider Vinegar Health Tonic: Mix with distilled water, raw honey and cayenne pepper for a general health tonic.

22. Jazz Up Tomato Juice: Add some zing by putting a shot (about 1 tablespoon) in your morning tomato juice. "This makes my home-made tomato juice really tangy every morning! YUM"

23. Cucumber Salad: Make a zippy cucumber salad with apple cider vinegar, chopped onions and mayo. – Audra P. (We like to use 2 cups sliced cucumbers, 2 tablespoons chopped onions, ½ cup mayo, and 1 tablespoon apple cider vinegar, plus salt and pepper.)

24. DIY Apple Cider Vinegar Shampoo: Create your own shampoo by adding 1 tablespoon to a cup of chamomile tea.

25. Smoothie-Booster: Add a shot to your green superfood smoothie for a nutritious recovery drink. "I use it in my smoothies…".

26. Fluffy Rice: Get fluffier rice by adding a splash (about 1 teaspoon) to rice water while cooking. "I LOVE this stuff!! I put a capful into my raw rice before cooking and it's nice and fluffy. No vinegar taste!!"

27. Apple Cider Vinegar Fruit & Veggie Scrub: Use it to clean fruits and vegetables before eating.

28. Detangle Children's Hair: Gently detangle children's long locks by adding a splash during final rinse.

29. Remove Rust/Mineral Stains: Place a cloth soaked in apple cider vinegar over rust or mineral stains and let it sit overnight to help remove stains.

30. Regular Vinegar Replacement: Replace regular vinegar with apple cider vinegar in all your recipes!

The Best Apple Cider Vinegar to Buy

The question of "what's the best" always comes up no matter what the topic of the day may be. What's the best apple cider vinegar for weight loss support? Which apple cider vinegar is best for hair and skin? What's the best tasting apple cider vinegar that's good for smoothies and detox drinks?

On the flip side, some people wonder "can apple cider vinegar be bad for me?" The caution comes with the acidic nature of ACV. If you're bold enough to drink it straight, it's still a good idea to dilute it a bit to keep your stomach happy.

I recommend buying an organic apple cider vinegar that is raw, unprocessed, unfiltered, unpasteurized and contains the mother. Here are top two recommended apple cider vinegar products.

1. Swanson Organic Apple Cider Vinegar with Mother

2. Bragg's Apple Cider Vinegar with Mother

These products are nearly identical and get our seal of approval for meeting our quality criteria listed above. Here is a quick comparison chart for these two apple cider vinegar products.

What is the Mother in Apple Cider Vinegar?

The apple cider vinegar mother is a natural complex of friendly bacteria, proteins, enzymes and fiber. Apple cider vinegar with mother gives the vinegar a cloudy appearance, but that's good – filtered, refined versions of apple cider vinegar that don't contain the mother are not as beneficial.

1. Apple Cider Vinegar Facial Toner

2. Apple Cider Vinegar All-Purpose Cleaner

3. Apple Cider Vinegar & Honey Vinaigrette

4. Apple Cider Vinegar Throat Soother

5. Apple Cider Vinegar Mocktail

Apple Cider Vinegar Recipes

Bragg's Apple Cider Vinegar and Swanson's Apple Cider Vinegar with Mother offer a wide range of health benefits, but there are only a select few who can handle drinking these apple cider vinegars straight. As an acidic product with no sweeteners, it can be very hard for anyone's palate to handle. But there are recipes that can either mask the flavor or work with the flavor to make a drink that is more appealing to the taste buds. The problem is that no two palates are the same, so it's difficult to say with certainty which apple cider vinegar recipe will taste the best to you.

Some people like to mix apple cider vinegar with other acidic juices like orange juice or flavors that are similarly acidic, while others just drink a shot of the apple cider vinegar and follow it with something else to mask the taste, like bread. It often takes some trial and error to see what works best for your palate, but here is an apple cider vinegar drink recipe you can start with.

Apple Cider Vinegar Mocktail Recipe – Detox Drink Recipe

Ingredients

- 2 tablespoon of apple cider vinegar to 8 ounces of water.
- 2 teaspoons organic honey
- 1 to 3 leaves of your favorite herb (like basil or mint
- 4 of your favorite berries like blueberries, strawberries or blackberries.

Instructions

Mix together and drink, or add the mocktail to your favorite smoothie recipe. You can also add 2 tablespoons of apple cider vinegar to your favorite fruit and vegetable juices or smoothie recipes.

Apple Cider Vinegar & Honey Vinaigrette – Salad Dressing Recipe

Try this awesome recipe for Apple Cider Vinegar and Honey Vinaigrette. Any combination of these ingredients would make a great salad, so feel free to adjust the recipe to your taste! It's perfect for lunch or dinner for two!

Dressing Ingredients

- 3/4 cup olive oil
- 1/4 cup apple cider vinegar
- 2 tablespoons water
- 2 tablespoons honey
- 1 1/2 teaspoons salt
- 1/4 teaspoon pepper

Salad Toppings

- 2 cups spinach
- 1 apple, chopped
- 2 tablespoons walnuts
- 2 tablespoons raisins
- 1 to 2 ounces of your favorite cheese, diced

Instructions

Combine apple cider vinegar, water, honey, salt and pepper in a blender. Drizzle olive oil into blender until combined. Combine dressing & toppings in a bowl; serve.

Apple Cider Vinegar Facial Toner

Try this easy facial toner.

Ingredients

- 1 part apple cider vinegar
- 4 parts water

Instructions

Mix together in a bowl and apply to skin with a cotton ball or washcloth. Rinse off with warm water after 10 minutes.

Apple Cider Vinegar Throat Soother

Ingredients

- 1/4 cup of Apple Cider Vinegar
- 1/4 cup warm water

Instructions

Mix together in a glass and use as a gargle once per hour or as needed for throat comfort.

Apple Cider Vinegar All-Purpose Cleaner

Ingredients

- 1 part water
- 1 part apple cider vinegar
- 3 drops of your favorite essential oil (like lavender, tea tree or lemon)

Instructions

Add the mix to a spray bottle and keep on hand for an all-purpose cleaner. Be sure to test surfaces by applying a small amount first before spraying and wiping clean.

CHAPTER 8

7 Side Effects of Too Much Apple Cider Vinegar

Apple cider vinegar is a natural tonic.

It has several health benefits that are supported by scientific studies in humans.

However, people have also raised concerns about its safety and possible side effects.

This section takes a look at apple cider vinegar's potential side effects.

It also provides instructions on how to consume apple cider vinegar safely.

Unfortunately, apple cider vinegar has been reported to cause some side effects.

This is particularly true in large doses.

Although small amounts are generally fine and healthy, taking too much can be harmful and even dangerous.

1. Delayed Stomach Emptying

Apple cider vinegar helps prevent blood sugar spikes by reducing the rate at which food leaves the stomach and enters the lower digestive tract. This slows down its absorption into the bloodstream.

However, this effect may worsen symptoms of gastroparesis, a common condition in people with type 1 diabetes.

In gastroparesis, the nerves in the stomach don't work properly, so food stays in the stomach too long and is not emptied at a normal rate.

Symptoms of gastroparesis include heartburn, bloating and nausea. For type 1 diabetics who have gastroparesis, timing insulin with meals is very challenging because it's hard to predict how long it will take food to be digested and absorbed.

One controlled study looked at 10 patients with type 1 diabetes and gastroparesis.

Drinking water with 2 tablespoons (30 ml) of apple cider vinegar significantly increased the amount of time that food stayed in the stomach, compared to drinking plain water.

2. Digestive Side Effects

Apple cider vinegar may cause unpleasant digestive symptoms in some people.

Human and animal studies have found that apple cider vinegar and acetic acid may decrease appetite and promote feelings of fullness, leading to a natural reduction in calorie intake.

However, one controlled study suggests that in some cases, appetite and food intake may decrease due to indigestion.

The people who consumed a drink containing 25 grams (0.88 oz) of apple cider vinegar reported less appetite but also significantly greater feelings of nausea, especially when the vinegar was part of an unpleasant-tasting drink.

3. Low Potassium Levels and Bone Loss

There are no controlled studies on apple cider vinegar's effects on blood potassium levels and bone health at this time.

However, there is one case report of low blood potassium and bone loss that was attributed to large doses of apple cider vinegar taken over a long period of time.

A 28-year-old woman consumed 8 oz (250 ml) of apple cider vinegar diluted in water on a daily basis for six years.

She was admitted to the hospital with low potassium levels and other abnormalities in blood chemistry.

What's more, the woman was diagnosed with osteoporosis, a condition of brittle bones that is rarely seen in young people.

Doctors who treated the woman believe the large daily doses of apple cider vinegar led to minerals being leached from her bones to buffer the acidity of her blood.

They also noted that high acid levels can reduce the formation of new bone.

Of course, the amount of apple cider vinegar in this case was much more than most people would consume in a single day — plus, she did this every day for many years.

4. Erosion of Tooth Enamel

Acidic foods and beverages have been shown to damage tooth enamel.

Soft drinks and fruit juices have been more widely studied, but some research shows the acetic acid in vinegar may also damage tooth enamel.

In one lab study, enamel from wisdom teeth was immersed in different vinegars with pH levels ranging from 2.7–3.95. The vinegars led to a 1–20% loss of minerals from the teeth after four hours.

Importantly, this study was done in a lab and not in the mouth, where saliva helps buffer acidity. Nevertheless, there's some evidence that large amounts of vinegar may cause dental erosion.

A case study also concluded that a 15-year-old girl's severe dental decay was caused by consuming one cup (237 ml) of undiluted apple cider vinegar per day as a weight loss aid.

5. Throat Burns

Apple cider vinegar has the potential to cause esophageal (throat) burns.

A review of harmful liquids accidentally swallowed by children found acetic acid from vinegar was the most common acid that caused throat burns.

Researchers recommended vinegar be considered a "potent caustic substance" and kept in childproof containers.

There are no published cases of throat burns from apple cider vinegar itself.

However, one case report found that an apple cider vinegar tablet caused burns after becoming lodged in a woman's throat. The woman said she experienced pain and difficulty swallowing for six months after the incident.

6. Skin Burns

Due to its strongly acidic nature, apple cider vinegar may also cause burns when applied to the skin.

In one case, a 14-year-old girl developed erosions on her nose after applying several drops of apple cider vinegar to remove two moles, based on a protocol she'd seen on the internet.

In another, a 6-year-old boy with multiple health problems developed leg burns after his mother treated his leg infection with apple cider vinegar.

There are also several anecdotal reports online of burns caused by applying apple cider vinegar to the skin.

7. Drug Interactions

A few medications may interact with apple cider vinegar:

- Diabetes medication: People who take insulin or insulin-stimulating medications and vinegar may experience dangerously low blood sugar or potassium levels.
- Digoxin (Lanoxin): This medication lowers your blood potassium levels. Taking it in combination with apple cider vinegar could lower potassium too much.
- Certain diuretic drugs: Some diuretic medications cause the body to excrete potassium. To prevent potassium levels from dropping too low, these drugs shouldn't be consumed with large amounts of vinegar.

Printed in Great Britain
by Amazon

66212356R00071